thecollective
Contemporary Styles Series

CD INCLUDED

T0039786

Contemporary Jazz Styles for the Drums

Part I by Peter Retzlaff
Part II by Ian Froman

thecollective is a world-class learning center for drumset players, percussionists, bassists, keyboardists and guitarists of all levels. We offer plans of study ranging from individual lessons and clinics to full-time programs of ten weeks to two years in length. If you're serious about becoming the best musician you can be, we're serious about helping you accomplish that goal.

541 Avenue of the Americas, New York, NY 10011
T: 212-741-0091

www.thecoll.com

Executive Producer – *Lauren Keiser*
Executive Co-producer – *John Castellano*
Author Liason – *Tony Maggiolino*
Creative Director – *Alex Teploff*
Managing Editor – *Nicholas Hopkins*
Production Editor – *Joe Bergamini*
Cover Design – *Andrew J. Dowty*
Book Design – *Andrew J. Dowty*
Production Designer – *Andy Ray Wong*
Photo of New York City – *Maureen Plainfield*
Other Photography – *Andy Dowty and Kyung Chul-Choi*
Production Coordinator and Audio Engineer – *Tony Conniff*

CARL FISCHER®
65 Bleecker Street, New York, NY 10012

ISBN 0-8258-6269-8

TABLE OF CONTENTS

Performers on the CD:

Part I by Peter Retzlaff:	**Part II by Ian Froman:**
Peter Retzlaff – Drums	Ian Froman – Drums
David Ambrosio – Bass	Joe Fitzgerald – Bass
Jacob Sacks – Piano	Bob Quaranta – Piano

FOREWORD

The Collective was established in 1977 by a small group of professional New York musicians, who wanted to pool their energies and create a place where young drummers, and later bass, guitar, and keyboard students, could study and prepare themselves for a career in music. Since opening its doors, The Collective has graduated thousands of students, who have gone on to establish themselves in the world of professional music. I don't think that it is immodest to say that our alumni are helping to shape the direction that popular music is taking around the world.

Over the years the curriculum at The Collective has evolved to include a wide range of courses focusing on everything from technique and reading, to the study of all the important contemporary and ethnic styles. This book, along with our other Rhythm Section based books, covers the material offered in the Collective's Certificate Program.

The styles offered here represent the key styles in the contemporary idiom. Since all styles have tended to grow out of each other, and mutually influence each other, the student will find common threads that link them all together and make it easier to absorb and make them part of a young musician's personal style signature.

Each book contains a brief biography of the author, who is the faculty member who teaches this style at The Collective. You will also find a brief introduction to the general style and examples of the various substyles to be studied. Woven throughout the material are performance tips that come out of the teacher's years of experience. The most important element, however, are the pre-recorded rhythm-section CDs, on which our teachers perform with other musicians who also specialize in playing the style. Listening to and practicing with these CDs are the most important things for you to do to develop skills playing in the style. Music notation and the written word can, at best, only help you derive an intellectual understanding of the music. It is in listening to the actual music that you will come to understand it. In this regard, we strongly encourage you to make an effort to listen to the music listed in the recommended discography at the end of each section. The blank staves are meant for you to notate your own personal variations for each style. First, you must learn the pure style; then, you can adapt it to your own musical needs.

I would like to express my appreciation to all the teachers who have, over the years, contributed to the growth of the Collective and to this program in particular. I would also like to thank the hard working and talented folks at Carl Fischer for supporting our effort to get it right, and doing such a fine job with this book. Finally, I would like to thank Tony Maggiolino of our staff for all his hard work in coordinating all the material, and struggling to meet ever looming deadlines.

—John Castellano.
Director, The Collective

PART I:
Peter Retzlaff

About Peter Retzlaff

Known for his musicality and command of a wide range of styles, Peter Retzlaff has played with Kenny Werner, Greg Osby, Diane Schuur, Ray Vega, the BMI Big Band, and Maynard Ferguson. As an educator, Peter has been an integral member of the Drummers Collective since 1995. He maintains an active private teaching schedule and has taught classes in Jazz, Rock, Funk, Brazilian, Afro-Cuban, Afro-Caribbean, Reading, Chart Interpretation, Rudiments, Technique, Odd Times, and Ensemble Performance. In addition, he teaches at The New School in New York City.

Peter received a B.A. in Jazz and Commercial Music and a B.A. in Business Administration from Capital University. He also received a M.M. in Jazz Studies from the Manhattan School of Music. Peter is a clinician for Zildjian, Remo and Vic Firth.

Acknowledgements

I would like to thank my family for supporting my musical endeavors from day one; my musician "family" from my first gig until now; my first teachers Bob Breithaupt and Stan Smith, who exposed me to a wider view of music and the world; John Riley and Justin DiCioccio, who furthered my skills and knowledge, and showed me how to get going in NYC; Kenny Washington for his big ears, great knowledge and passion for this music; Ed Soph for his great concepts; Billy Hart for his wisdom in all aspects of life, music and otherwise; Zildjian, Remo and Vic Firth for their great products and support; the Collective staff and faculty; former Drummers Collective teachers Michael Lauren and Memo Acevedo; Jacob and Dave for their great playing and vibes; Kasia, Tony, and Joe for their efforts on this project; and to the past and present masters of this music. A big thanks to all of my students over the years: you have taught me more than I have taught you!

Author's Introduction

Jazz in the mid-1940s through the late 1950s was an exciting time, particularly for the drums. During this period, Bebop, Hard Bop, and Cool jazz styles emerged. Artists such as Dizzy Gillespie, Charlie Parker, Thelonious Monk, Bud Powell, Horace Silver, Miles Davis, Art Blakey and the Jazz Messengers, Sonny Rollins, and many others contributed to the evolution of jazz. By the late 1950s, John Coltrane and Ornette Coleman demonstrated new, more modern possibilities for jazz music.

In this era, small groups gained popularity. The melodies and harmonies of the compositions as well as the solos evolved to new levels of sophistication. Drumming also changed during this period. The ride cymbal became the main time-keeping device. The time feel grew lighter and more complex. Independence and coordination increased, and accompaniment became more active and interactive. The cymbals grew larger, while the drums became smaller. Listen to the drumming of Sid Catlett, Kenny Clarke, Max Roach, Art Blakey, Philly Joe Jones, Roy Haynes, Art Taylor, Jimmy Cobb, and Billy Higgins to gain insight into the drum innovations during this time.

Jazz, like all music, is a language. The more we immerse ourselves in a language, the more fluent we become. Practicing with books and CDs, watching videos and live performances, and working out technical issues on our instruments are all ways to become fluent in the language of music.

Working on technical patterns enables a student to increase coordination and independence skills. However, studying and practicing technical patterns alone do not compensate for the learning that takes place in a musical setting. We need to work on both technical and musical concepts at all times!

During the 1940s and 1950s, there were certain vocabulary phrases that were commonly used in the language of drumming. The vocabulary phrases contained in this book are ones that I find particularly helpful, especially when practiced and used in a musical context. By memorizing and combining these phrases while understanding their place within the music, you will become a better drummer and musician. Take your time absorbing this material, and have fun during this process.

Practicing with a Metronome

A jazz drummer needs to play smooth and comfortable time at a wide variety of tempos. Practice your time by playing with a metronome as well as with recordings.

Try this approach:

Days 1, 3, 5	Days 2, 4, 6
♩ = 60	♩ = 55
♩ = 70	♩ = 65
♩ = 80	♩ = 75
♩ = 90	♩ = 85
...up to your fastest comfortable tempo	...up to your fastest comfortable tempo

By varying the metronome markings by five beats per minute on alternate days, we double the number of tempos covered. Discover which tempos seem naturally easy. Also, find the tempos that are difficult to feel and "hold onto."

Check your ability to remain steady first by playing time with the metronome. Then, turn it off while continuing to play. After a few minutes, turn it back on. Did your tempo move while the metronome was off, or did it remain steady? Experiment with the metronome, playing on quarter notes, on beats 2 and 4, on beats 1 and 3, and only on beat 1.

Recordings

Listening to recordings is a very important step in becoming a better drummer and musician. Listen to the great musicians for their vocabulary, feel, sound, touch, and vibe. Listen to one song many times. With each listen you should focus on:

1. The ride cymbal (the patterns, sound, feel and timbre of the cymbal).
2. The snare drum and bass drum comping (the patterns, sound, pitch and timbre of the drums).
3. The hi-hat (the **2** and **4** pattern as well as the comping patterns, and the sound and timbre of the hi-hat).
4. The dynamic build of the drummer within the music.
5. The drum patterns that outline, complement, and set up the melody of the song.
6. The drum patterns that outline the musical structure of the song.
7. The drummer's interaction with the rhythm section.
8. The drummer's interaction with the soloist.
9. Brush patterns.
10. The solo vocabulary and phrasing of the drummer.

Also, listen to the other players of the group. Listen to:

1. The bass player (the sound, feel, patterns, and connection with the drummer and band).
2. The chordal instruments, which can include piano, guitar, and vibraphone (comping, solo patterns, and interaction).
3. The main soloists (busy or spacious lines, solo development, interaction with rhythm section).

4. The rhythm section, which can include drums, bass, piano, guitar and vibraphone (interaction and connection with each other and with the soloist).

A drummer should also play along with music. Playing with recordings is a great way to experience the drummer's role in the band. This step is critical to musical development. Spend at least one-third of your practice time playing with music.

Finally, transcribe vocabulary patterns of the great musicians. Listen to music to find patterns that you want to use. Write down the cymbal, snare, bass, hi-hat, and solo patterns.

The Ride-Cymbal Pattern

From the middle of the 1940s, through middle to late 1950s, drummers played in a repeated ride-cymbal style most of the time. The repeated cymbal pattern looks like this:

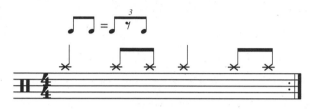

Innovators such as Kenny Clarke, Max Roach, Philly Joe Jones, and Art Blakey demonstrated this concept in their playing during this time period. The players did vary their patterns, but used the repeated ride pattern most often.

By the late 1950s, drummers such as Jimmy Cobb and Elvin Jones began to play more quarter notes in their cymbal patterns with some eighth-note skips added to round out the feeling of the pattern. Listen to Jimmy's playing on the Miles Davis album *Kind of Blue* to hear this stylistic change. By the 1960s, all of the major innovators made the transition to this style. Today, a drummer is expected to play the ride cymbal in this manner. However, the student should practice both types of cymbal concepts. In this book, the $\frac{4}{4}$ and $\frac{3}{4}$ sections contain both repeated and non-repeated vocabulary patterns.

The Role of the Components of the Drumset

It is important to understand how each part of the drumset supports and complements the music. The ride cymbal and the upright (or acoustic) bass provide the propulsion and cushion for the band to flow over. This ride-cymbal/acoustic-bass connection is what the other band members feel the most. Many drummers play a soft quarter-note bass drum pattern with the ride cymbal and snare drum comping. This technique is called "feathering" the bass drum, and its purpose is to add some low end or weight to the groove. It is "felt," rather than heard. The feathered bass-drum note is played one to two inches from the drumhead.

The snare drum and bass drum comping variations provide a syncopated push within the drumset groove. To syncopate means to place notes on the unexpected, weak, or offbeat parts of the measure. Jazz songs, solos, and the rhythm section accompaniments all utilize this syncopated concept. The snare and bass comping (along with the piano and guitar) utilize both upbeat and downbeat patterns. However, there are a greater percentage of upbeats in most players' vocabulary. Study recordings and hear how experienced rhythm-section players phrase their comping within a musical context.

The hi-hat pattern, played on beats 2 and 4, adds swing to the ride-cymbal pattern. Hi-hat patterns played on other parts of the beat act as comping notes within the groove.

Dynamic Development

In a band context, the drummer must use dynamics to shape the music. We must practice dynamics just as we practice time and vocabulary.

As an exercise, play time within a musical structure such as a twelve-measure blues or a thirty-two measure AABA song form. Sing a simple melody or hear the chords as you play. Start softly, and gradually increase the volume and intensity of your time. Practice shifting dynamics, such as p to mf, p to mp, p to f, p to ff, within one chorus or several choruses. Also, practice shorter bursts of volume and intensity. Practice this concept in four- and eight-measure segments.

In addition, practice increasing the density of your comping figures. Start out with ride-cymbal and hi-hat time. Gradually add snare and bass patterns over one or several choruses to increase intensity.

Finally, listen to hear how the great drummers shaped the music. Art Blakey and Philly Joe Jones were masters of these concepts; listen to their playing to better understand dynamic development.

Learning Songs

It is essential that a drummer learn the important songs in the jazz tradition. It is very difficult to play music with a band without this knowledge. A drummer must know and be able to sing the melody of any song he plays. In addition, the drummer must be able to hear the harmonic movement of the chord progression. By knowing the melody and harmony, the drummer can hear where he is in the form of the song during the melody as well as during the solos. Remember that music is made up of melody, harmony, and rhythm, and we need to be versed in all of these areas. Study some piano, guitar, or vibraphone. These instruments give you insight into these three components of music.

Set-up

The typical jazz drumset includes a bass drum (18 to 20 inches), tom-toms (12 and 14 inches), a snare drum (14 inches), hi-hats, a ride cymbal and a crash cymbal. The typical jazz-drum tuning can be high or low in pitch, but the fundamental sound needs to be resonant with good sustain. This jazz-drum sound blends well with the upright bass and other acoustic instruments of the jazz ensemble.

Jazz cymbals have more "wash" and less "ping" than rock cymbals. This sound also blends better with the jazz ensemble. Common ride-cymbal sizes are 20 and 22 inches. Some crash-cymbal sizes are 16, 17, or 18 inches. In some cases, a jazz drummer may only use two ride cymbals (without crash cymbals). This works because the cymbals are thin enough to act as both a crash and a ride cymbal.

Drumkey Notation

CHAPTER 1:

Jazz $\frac{4}{4}$ Time: Repeated Ride-Coordination/Vocabulary Comping Patterns

Play the comping notes on the snare drum:

1. with no bass drum.
2. with feathered bass drum on quarter notes.

Next, play the comping notes on the bass drum. Then alternate the comping notes between the snare drum and bass drum. Make sure you memorize the comping patterns and play the hi-hat on beats 2 and 4.

Upbeat Patterns

Downbeat Patterns

Another View: Comping Notes Only

Eventually, you should play these figures without having to see the ride-cymbal pattern written out above them. Here are the same comping patterns written out without the cymbal.

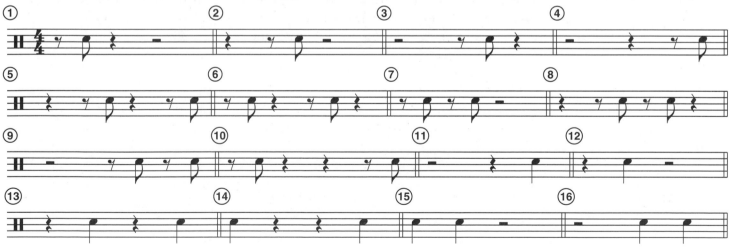

You can add variety to the sound of the snare drum. Play comping patterns at a:

1. Soft sound level (1 inch from the drum head).
2. Medium sound level (2 to 3 inches from the drum head).
3. Loud sound level (4 to 5 inches from the drum head).

Also, try playing with a buzz stroke and a soft rim shot. Mix these sounds within your comping patterns. Once you gain control of these different comping exercises, play along with the $\frac{4}{4}$ CD tracks numbers 14 and 16.

Repeated Ride Comping-Combinations:

Play as:

1. two-measure combinations
2. four-measure combinations
3. eight-measure combinations
4. twelve-measure combination
5. sixteen-measure combinations

Play the comping notes in the:

1. Snare drum
2. Bass drum

Alternate the figures in the snare drum and bass drum. Improvise the figures in the snare drum and bass drum. Memorize the combinations. Play the hi-hat on beats 2 and 4

Once you gain control of these combinations, play along with the $\frac{4}{4}$ CD tracks numbers 14 and 16.

Multiple-Note Comping Patterns

Play comping notes on the snare drum:

1. with no bass drum.
2. with feathered bass drum.

Again, memorize the comping patterns and play the hi-hat on beats 2 and 4.

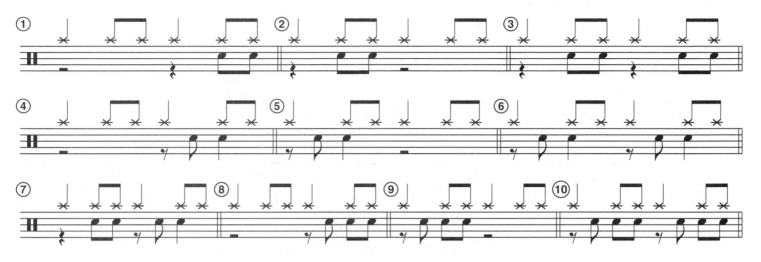

After getting comfortable with the above patterns, split them up between snare drum and bass drum. Here are some examples.

Another View: Comping Notes Only

These are the same rhythms as above, written out without the ride-cymbal pattern.

Once you gain control of these comping exercises, play along with the $\frac{4}{4}$ CD tracks numbers 14 and 16.

CHAPTER 2

Jazz $\frac{4}{4}$ Time: Basic Non-Repeated Jazz Ride Vocabulary

The repeated jazz pattern is:

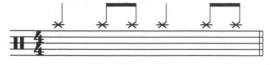

Some basic variations:

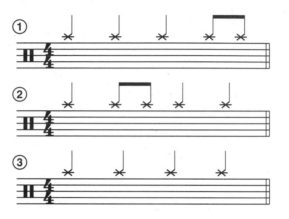

These patterns omit one or two of the repeated ride skip beats. Memorize these four cymbal vocabulary patterns.

$\frac{4}{4}$ Basic Non-Repeated Ride-Cymbal Combinations

Play with:

1. Feathered bass drum
2. No bass drum

Play the hi-hat on beats 2 and 4

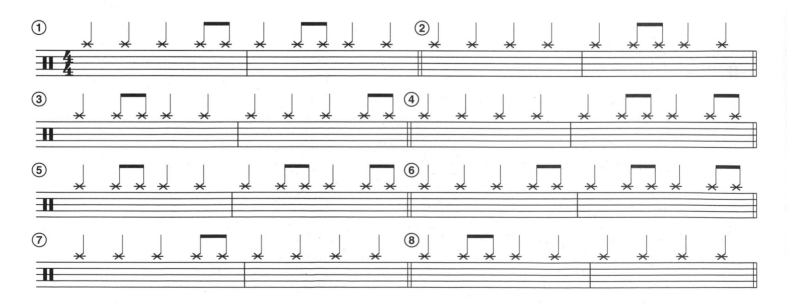

$\frac{4}{4}$ Basic Non-Repeated Ride Cymbal/Comping Patterns

Play comping notes on the snare drum:

1. with no bass drum.
2. with feathered bass drum.

Next, play comping notes between the bass drum. Then, alternate the comping notes in the snare drum and bass drum. Make sure you memorize the ride cymbal comping patterns and play the hi-hat on beats 2 and 4.

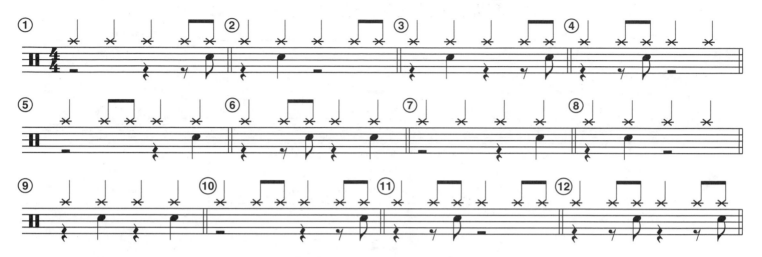

$\frac{4}{4}$ Basic Ride Cymbal/Comping Combinations

Play as two-measure combinations and play as four-measure combinations.

Play the comping notes on the snare drum:

1. with no bass drum.
2. With feathered bass drum

Play the comping notes on the bass drum. Also alternate the comping notes between the snare drum and bass drum. Finally, improvise the comping notes between the snare drum and bass drum. Remember to play the hi-hat on beats 2 and 4.

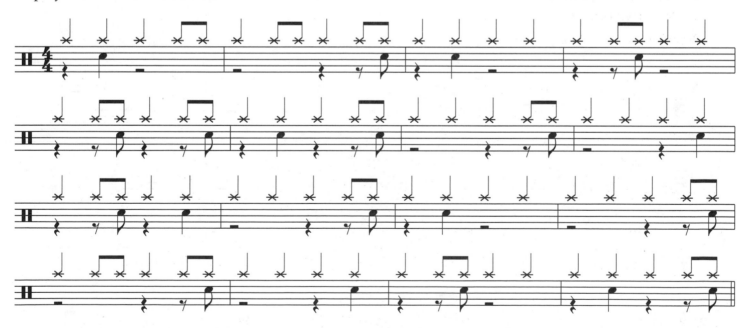

Once you gain control of these comping exercises, play along with the $\frac{4}{4}$ CD tracks numbers 14 and 16.

Advanced Ride-Cymbal Patterns with Comping Notes

These patterns are part of the more complex vocabulary used in this era. I have included upbeat comping notes with each cymbal phrase.

Play the comping notes on the:

1. snare drum.
2. bass drum.
3. snare drum and bass drum, alternating the figures.

Also, improvise the upbeat snare-drum and bass-drum combinations. Play the hi-hat on beats 2 and 4. Memorize these patterns.

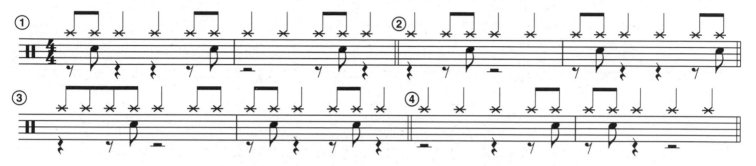

Here is a sixteen-measure phrase.

Play the comping notes on the:

1. snare drum.
2. bass drum.

Next, alternate the comping notes between the snare drum and bass drum. Finally, improvise the comping notes between the snare drum and bass drum.

CHAPTER 3:
Feathering the Bass Drum

Practice playing the ride cymbal (repeated or non-repeated patterns) with the hi-hat on beats 2 and 4. Add the feathered bass-drum pattern. Play the bass drum 1 to 2 inches from the head.

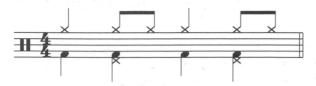

The bass drum pattern should be felt rather than heard. It takes much practice to gain control of this technique.

Once this pattern becomes more comfortable, try adding some louder bass-drum notes. To play upbeat bass-drum accents, omit the next downbeat note before starting the feathered pattern again. For example:

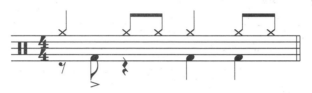

To play downbeat bass drum accents, you can play or omit the next downbeat note before starting the feathered pattern again.

Sixteen-Measure Feathered/Accent Bass-Drum Exercise

Play the hi-hat on beats 2 and 4. Unaccented notes are one to two inches from the heads, *pp*.

After you gain some control of these bass-drum patterns, add some snare comping notes, but remember to play the hi-hat on beats 2 and 4.

For example:

Practice the feathered bass-drum style during the "4-feel" comping sections on the $\frac{4}{4}$ CD track numbers 14 and 16.

Playing "In 2" or "2-Feel"

When the band plays "In 2" or with a "2-feel", the bass player plays half-note time instead of quarter-note time. The drummer can play a "2-feel" several ways. First, the drummer can play with brushes, using a regular $\frac{4}{4}$ pattern. Or, the drummer can play open/closed hi-hat. The basic hi-hat pattern is:

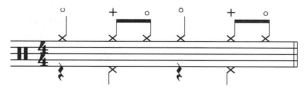

Some hi-hat embellishments are:

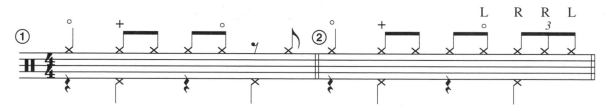

The drummer can also play the "2-feel" on the ride cymbal. The basic pattern is:

Some ride variations are:

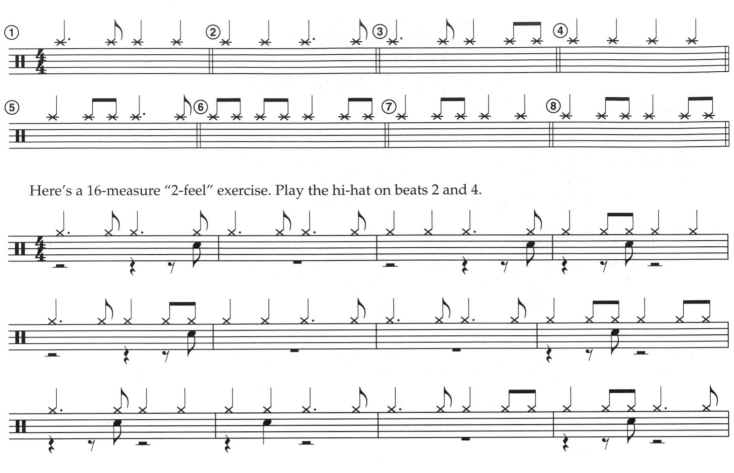

Here's a 16-measure "2-feel" exercise. Play the hi-hat on beats 2 and 4.

Practice the "2-feel" comping sections with the $\frac{4}{4}$ CD track numbers 14 and 16.

CHAPTER 4:
Jazz ¾ Time: Repeated Ride

The repeated ride pattern for ¾ time is:

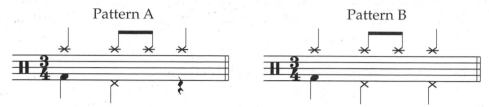

Pattern A · · · · · · · · · · · · · Pattern B

Notice the feel and sound difference between the two foot patterns. The two-note pattern (pattern A) conveys a greater sense of space in the groove. Play the bass drum at a soft dynamic level on beat one of the measure.

Practice foot patterns A and B. Play comping patterns on the:

1. snare drum.
2. bass drum, while keeping hi-hat patterns A and B consistent, as written above.
3. Play eighth notes on the snare drum, quarter notes on the bass drum.

¾ Repeated Ride-Coordination/Vocabulary Comping Patterns

¾ Repeated Ride Combinations

Play as a:

1. two-measure combination.
2. four-measure combination.
3. eight-measure combination.
4. twelve-measure combination.
5. sixteen-measure combination.

Play the comping notes on the:

1. snare drum with the foot patterns A and B.
2. bass drum, keeping hi-hat patterns A and B as written on top of p. 19.

Alternate the figures between the snare drum and bass drum. Make sure you memorize these combinations.

Play with the ¾ CD track number 18.

CHAPTER 5:
Jazz $\frac{3}{4}$ Time: Non-Repeated Jazz Ride Vocabulary

Play each cymbal pattern with foot patterns A and B (see p. 19). Again, memorize these cymbal patterns

$\frac{3}{4}$ Non-Repeated Jazz Ride Vocabulary/Comping Patterns

22

¾ Non-Repeated Ride Combinations

Play as a:

1. two-measure combination.
2. four-measure combination.
3. eight-measure combination.
4. twelve-measure combination.
5. sixteen-measure combination.

Play the comping notes in the:

1. snare drum with foot patterns A and B.
2. bass drum with hi-hat patterns A and B.

Alternate the figures between the snare drum and bass drum. Try to improvise the figures between the snare drum and bass drum.

Play with the ¾ CD track number 18.

CO7

CHAPTER 6:
Brushes

Brushes are an alternative way to play jazz time and solos. They can contribute a different musical color within the band context. Brushes can be used at a variety of tempos and dynamics levels. To achieve more volume, press the sweeping brush pattern into the head. Louder players often press the brush all the way to the back of the handle. To play softly, play the sweep on the front tip of the brush. If the lead hand plays a tap within the pattern, vary the dynamic level by raising or lowering the brush height, while adjusting the amount of wrist snap used. Practice the sweep motion to gain sound consistency. Also, play the brushes at a variety of tempos; the patterns must be played smaller as the tempo increases. Listen to the great players for their sound, feel, and touch. Once the basic patterns are learned, feel free to improvise the ride patterns as you would on the cymbal.

> ### Standard 4/4 Pattern
> *CD Track #1*

Standard $\frac{4}{4}$ Pattern

Left hand moves in a straight line.

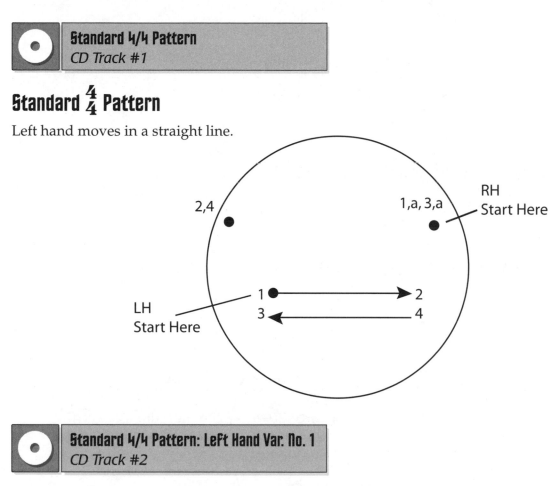

> ### Standard 4/4 Pattern: Left Hand Var. No. 1
> *CD Track #2*

Standard $\frac{4}{4}$ Pattern: Left Hand Variation No. 1

Left hand moves in a clockwise direction.

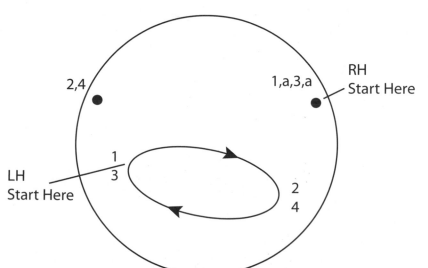

Standard 4/4 Pattern: Left Hand Var. No. 2
CD Track #3

Standard $\frac{4}{4}$ Pattern: Left Hand Variation No. 2

Left hand moves in a counter-clockwise direction.

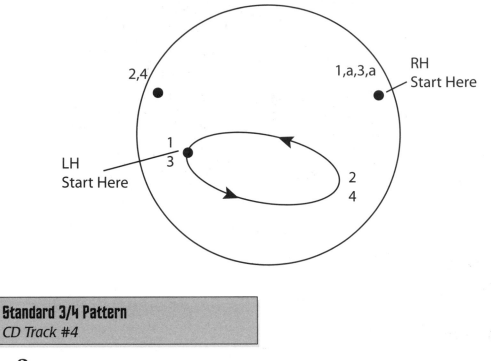

Standard 3/4 Pattern
CD Track #4

Standard $\frac{3}{4}$ Pattern

Both hands are reversed in the second measure. If the right hand pattern is awkward to play, keep your right hand on the right side of the drum.

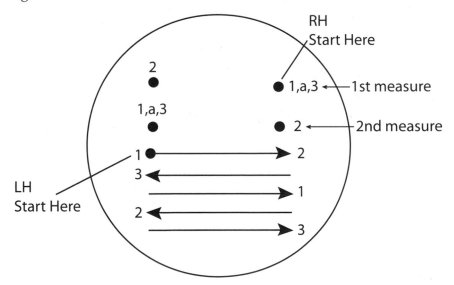

The left hand can also utilize an oval sweep motion as used in the $\frac{4}{4}$ left-hand variation on p. 23.

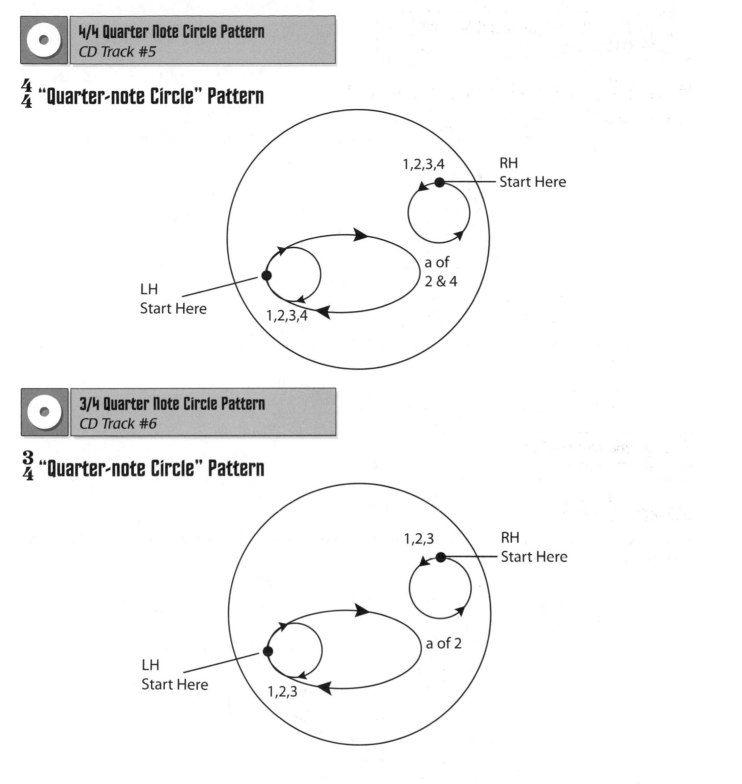

⁴⁄₄ "Quarter-note Circle" Pattern

³⁄₄ "Quarter-note Circle" Pattern

Left Hand Fill In
CD Track #7

Left Hand Fill-In

At slower tempos, the right hand can slide upward to mask the left-hand motion in the air. Left hand taps on "a" of 1 and 3. It slides on 2 and 4.

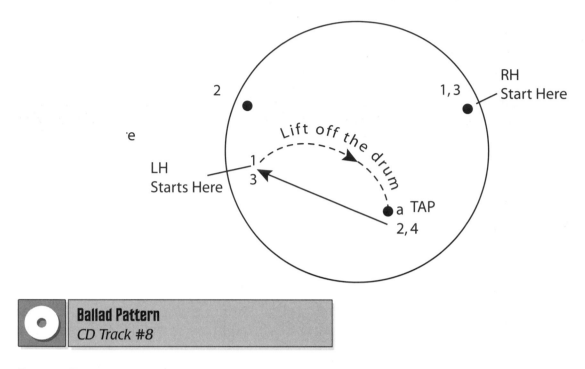

Ballad Pattern
CD Track #8

Ballad Pattern

Both hands sweep one circle per quarter note.

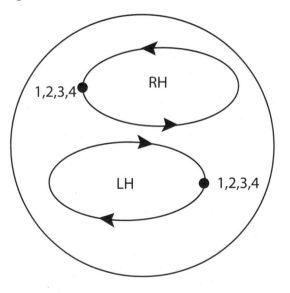

Switching From Brushes to Sticks

We need to be able to switch from brushes to sticks during the course of a song. Switch in the last measure of the musical phrase, so the stick hits the ride cymbal on beat 1, measure 1 of the new phrase.

Practice playing three measures of time followed by the switch in the fourth measure.

Switching to Sticks in 4/4 Time
CD Track #9

In $\frac{4}{4}$ time:

Brush time — Switch to sticks — New Phrase: Cymbal time

Switching to Sticks in 3/4 Time
CD Track #10

In $\frac{3}{4}$ time:

Brush time — Switch to sticks — New Phrase: Cymbal time

To play the switch, we can:

1. Keep the hi-hat going on beats 2 and 4 in $\frac{4}{4}$ time, or on beats 2 and 3 in $\frac{3}{4}$ time.
2. Splash the hi-hat on beats 2 and 4 in $\frac{4}{4}$ time, or on beats 2 and 3 in $\frac{3}{4}$ time.
3. Play a syncopated figure in the left hand while keeping the hi-hat going.

For example:

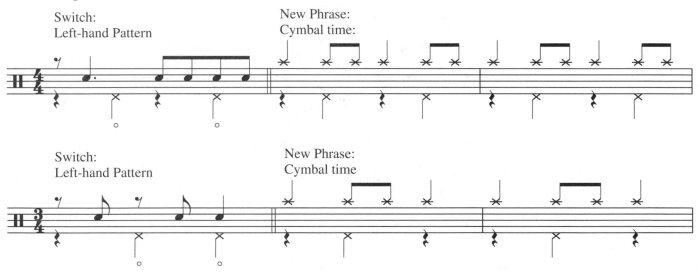

In this last measure, put down the brush on the floor tom, pick up the stick, and begin the ride pattern. Once the cymbal pattern is going, switch the other hand. I often rest the brushes on the rim of the floor tom so I can play this drum also.

When switching from sticks to brushes, quickly place both sticks on the floor tom, and then pick up both brushes at once. Play the hi-hat during the switch (either with a chick or splash sound).

CHAPTER 7:
Solo Vocabulary

Think of your solo vocabulary as words that need to be combined to make musical phrases. As a first step, learn some of the patterns. Play the vocabulary in a relaxed manner, and memorize the patterns. Start slowly, and build speed and accuracy by playing the vocabulary every time you practice.

After you have internalized a group of "words," begin using the patterns in the context of trading solos. In the jazz tradition, the drummer often trades solos with the other jazz musicians. The trades usually take place just before the last time the melody is played (the "head"). These trades can be four, eight, twelve, sixteen, or even thirty-two measures in length, and they follow the structure of the composition.

Initially, practice trading fours with yourself, playing four measures of jazz time followed by four measures of drum solo. As with jazz time, practice at a variety of tempos with the metronome. After you gain some skill with four-measure trades, experiment with trades that are eight and twelve measures in length. Eight-measure trades are often used in songs that have eight-measure sections. A popular song-form with this structure is the thirty-two-measure AABA form. Twelve-measure trades are often used with the blues song form.

Sometimes, the length of the trades change; one chorus may contain eight-measure trades, the next one four-measure trades. Also, the band could stop at the beginning of the chorus. In this instance, the drummer is expected to solo on the entire song form, guiding the band back into the melody when he or she is done. This solo on the entire form could be one or more choruses. Knowing the melody and harmony is the key to keeping your place in the song structure while trading solos.

Finally, practice playing the rhythm of a song melody on the drumset. This exercise helps you to become a more melodic drum soloist. Voice the melody around the drums. Practice combining vocabulary phrases with melody phrases in your solos.

$\frac{4}{4}$ Solo Vocabulary

Eighth-note Vocabulary

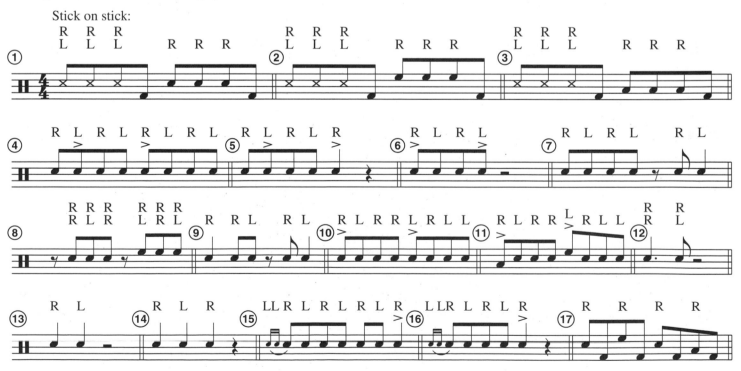

Two-measure Combinations

Triplet Vocabulary

Two-measure Combinations

Sixteenth-Note Vocabulary

Two-measure Combinations

Play this pattern with a straight eighth-note feel.

Solo Combinations

Here are some four-bar solo phrase ideas, constructed from the above.

Solo Combinations
CD Track #11

¾ Solo Vocabulary

Eighth-note Vocabulary

Triplet-note Vocabulary

Sixteenth-note Vocabulary

¾ Solo Combinations

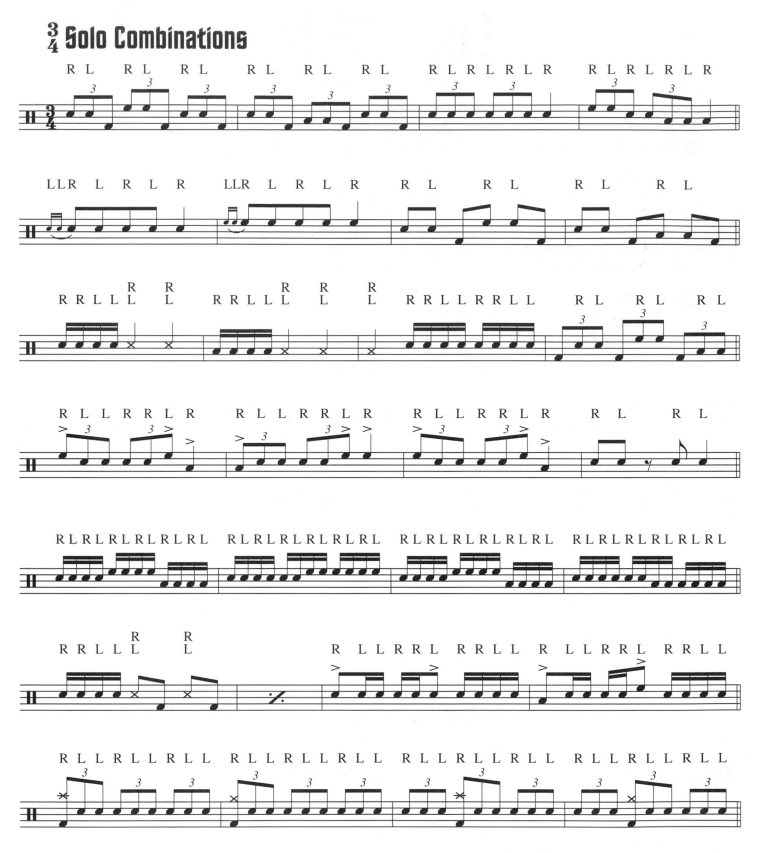

CHAPTER 8:
Turnarounds

Turnarounds are syncopated figures played at the end of the musical phrase. When the drummer plays a turnaround figure, the band feels the structure of the song. When playing the blues, the turnaround is played in measure 12 of the form. When playing a thirty-two-bar form, the turnaround is played in measure 32 of the form.

Within the turnaround figures in this book, there is a snare-drum/bass-drum combination followed by a crash on the ride cymbal with the shoulder of the stick. The crash is played on beat 4 or on the upbeat of beat 4, depending on the figure. Avoid playing crashes on beat 1 when playing a turnaround figure; beat 1 crashes stop the forward flow and momentum of a jazz song. When practicing these phrases, play three measures of time followed by the turnaround figure. Use a metronome to check your accuracy. Also, play with the CDs, adding turnarounds at the end of the song form.

Play the hi-hat on beats 2 and 4.

Turnarounds
CD Track #12

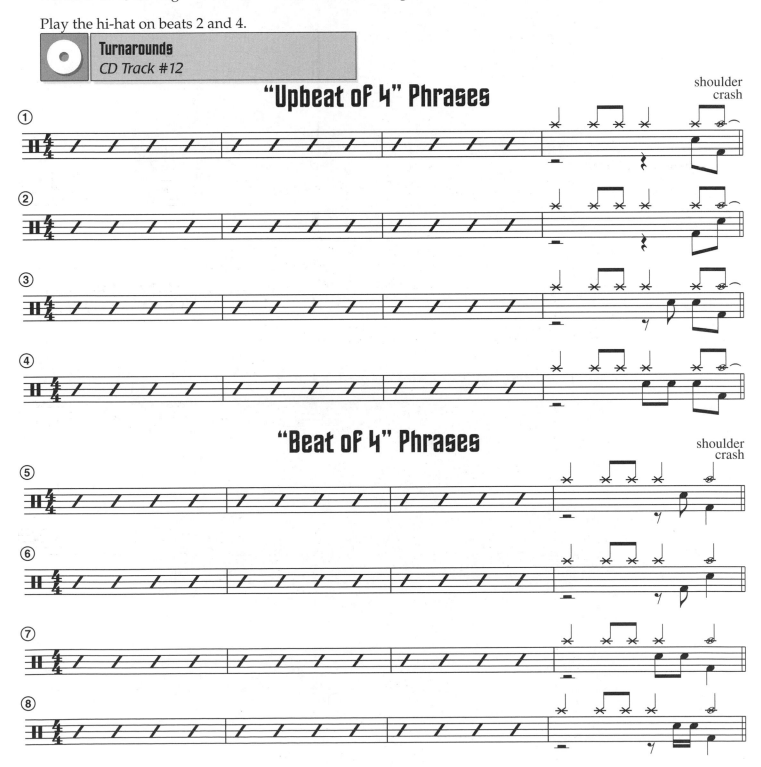

Philly Joe Jones Turnaround Phrase

Art Blakey Turnaround Phrase

This pattern was created by Philly Joe Jones. Listen to Miles Davis' CD *Milestones* to hear it performed.

PLAY-ALONG TRACKS:

Blues Tune
CD Track #13 (Demo)/#14 (Play-along)

Blues Tune

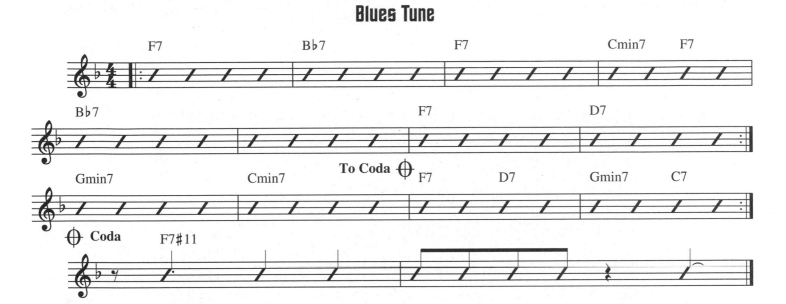

Form:

1. The piano comps and the bass and drums play with a "2-feel"; two choruses.
2. The piano solos and the bass and drums play with a "4-feel"; four choruses.
3. The piano comps and the bass and drums play with a "2-feel"; one chorus (go to the coda).

Rythm Changes Tune
CD Track #15 (Demo)/#16 (Play-along)

Rhythm Changes Tune

Form:

1. The piano comps and the bass and drums play with a "2-feel"; one chorus.
2. The piano solos and the bass and drums play with a "4-feel"; three choruses.
3. The piano comps and the bass and drums play with a "2-feel" in the A sections and with a "4-feel" in the B section (go to the coda).

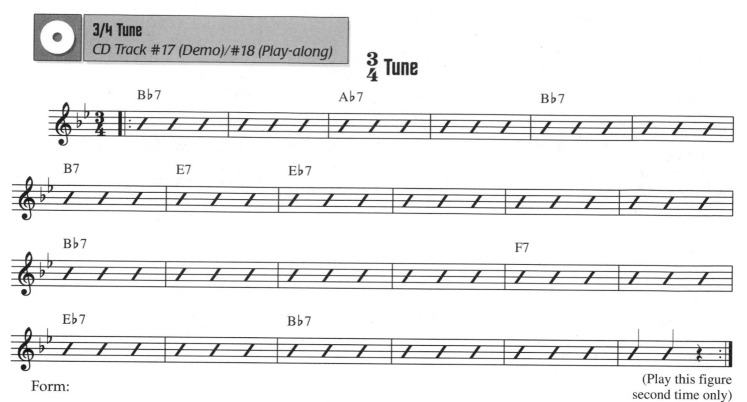

3/4 Tune
CD Track #17 (Demo)/#18 (Play-along)

(Play this figure
second time only)

Form:

1. The piano comps and the bass and drums play time; one chorus.
2. The piano solos and the bass and drums play time; four choruses.
3. The piano comps and the bass and drums play time; one chorus (to the end).

Here are lists of $\frac{4}{4}$ and $\frac{3}{4}$ songs:

$\frac{4}{4}$ time

Airegin
All of You
Along Came Betty
Anthropology
Au Privave
Billie's Bounce
Blues for Alice
Blues March
Blue Monk
Blue Seven
Bye-Bye Blackbird
Cherokee
Confirmation
Daahoud
Donna Lee
Doodlin'
Four
Freddie Freeloader
Giant Steps
If I Were a Bell
I'll Remember April
In Walked Bud
Jordu
Joy Spring
Milestones
Moment's Notice
Mr. PC
Night in Tunisia, A
Now's the Time
Oleo
On Green Dolphin Street
Ornithology
Pent-up House
Rhythm-A-Ning
Scrapple from the Apple
So What
Stablemates
Star Eyes
Straight No Chaser
Tune up
Walkin'
Well You Needn't
What Is This Thing Called Love?
Whisper Not
Woody 'n' You

$\frac{3}{4}$ Time

Alice in Wonderland
All Blues
Bluesette
Someday My Prince Will
Come
Tenderly
Up Jumped Spring
Valse Hot
West Coast Blues

Selected Discography

Blakey, Art	Art Blakey and the Jazz Messengers:
	Moanin'
	Mosaic
	The Big Beat
Catlett, Sid	Dizzy Gillespie: *Groovin' High*
Clarke, Kenny	Miles Davis: *Walkin'*
Cobb, Jimmy	Miles Davis: *Kind of Blue*
	Wynton Kelly Trio with Wes Montgomery: *Smokin' at the Half Note*
Dunlop, Frankie	Thelonious Monk:
	Monk's Dream
	Criss Cross
Haynes, Roy	Thelonious Monk :
	In Action
	Misterioso
	Roy Haynes: *Out of the Afternoon*
Higgins, Billy	Ornette Coleman: *The Shape of Jazz to Come*
	Lee Morgan: *The Sidewinder*
Jones, Philly Joe	Miles Davis: *Milestones*
	John Coltrane: *Blue Train*
Roach, Max	Charlie Parker: *Best of the Complete Savoy and Dial Studio Recordings*
	Clifford Brown and Max Roach:
	At Basin Street
	Clifford Brown and Max Roach
Taylor, Art	John Coltrane: *Giant Steps*
Wilson, Shadow	Thelonious Monk Quartet with John Coltrane: *At Carnegie Hall*

Recommended Books and Videos

Drumset Books

Chapin, Jim. *Advanced Techniques for the Modern Drummer*

Hart, Billy. *Jazz Drumming*

Lacinak, Chris. *A Modern Approach to New Orleans Drumming*

Moore, Stanton. *Take It to the Street*

Ramsay, John. *Art Blakey's Jazz Messages*

———. *The Drummer's Complete Vocabulary as Taught by Alan Dawson*

Reed, Ted. *Syncopation*

Riley, Herlin and Vidacovich, Johnny. *New Orleans Jazz and Second Line Drumming*

Riley, John. *The Art of Bop Drumming*

———. *Beyond Bop Drumming*

———. *The Jazz Drummer's Workshop*

Snidero, Jim. *Jazz Conception for Drums*

Soph, Ed. *Musical Time*

Snare Drum Books

Cirone, Anthony. *Portraits in Rhythm*

Morello, Joe. *Master Studies*

Stone, George Lawrence. *Stick Control*

Wilcoxin, Charles S. *Modern Rudimental Swing Solos*

———. *All American Drummer*

Textbooks

Gridley, Mark. *Jazz Styles*

Hunt, Joe. *52nd Street Beat*

Videos

New Orleans Drumming (Alfred)

Legends of Jazz Drumming Part I: 1920–1950 (Alfred)

Legends of Jazz Drumming Part II: 1950–1970 (Alfred)

PART II:
Ian Froman

About Ian Froman

A seasoned creative and working musician, Ian moved to the United States from Ottawa, Canada, where he began playing drums in his early teens. His studies in jazz performance began at the Berklee College of Music (B.M. 1984; selected to attend the Atlantic Center for the Arts in Florida to study with Elvin Jones) and then continued with Miroslav Vitous and Bob Moses at the New England Conservatory of Music (M.M. 1984). Ian is an Associate Professor at the Berklee College of Music, adjunct faculty member at the New School University and a faculty member at the Drummers Collective.

Ian lives in New York City, where he has performed and recorded with many of the city's top artists. His extensive touring in North America, Europe and Asia has included club, concert and festival appearances. He has also appeared on television and radio broadcasts with such artists as John Abercrombie, Arild Anderson, Jerry Bergonzi, Michael Brecker, Gary Burton, Marc Copeland, Garry Dial, George Garzone, Larry Goldings, Mick Goodrick, Larry Grenadier, Tim Hagans, Craig Handy, Ratzo Harris, John Hart, Kevin Hayes, Dave Holland, Dave Lieman, Rick Margitza, Cecil McBee, Ron McClure, Ben Monder, George Mraz, Lonnie Plaxico, Mike Stern, John Taylor, Miroslav Vitous and Kenny Wheeler. He has received two Canadian Juno Awards (1998 and 1999), two Jazz Report Magazine Awards (1998 and 1999), and a West Coast Music Award (1998) for his work with the Canadian group Metalwood.

Author's Introduction

Part II covers the continuation of the straight-ahead and bebop jazz styles discussed in Part I of this book. As the style progressed from the 1950s into the 1960s, drummers such as Roy Haynes, Jimmy Cobb and Joe Chambers developed new ways of riding the cymbal and comping. Elvin Jones and Tony Williams were the major influences of the 1960s, leading the way for Jack DeJohnette to bring the style into present-day drumming, influencing the likes of Jeff Watts, Bill Stewart and Brian Blade.

Developments in $\frac{4}{4}$ swing, $\frac{3}{4}$ swing and straight-eighth styles will be covered in this section.

General Performance Tips

The "Balance of Sound" changed dramatically in this style of drumming, as the ride cymbal became the primary voice of the drumset. The snare drum, bass drum and hi-hat became equal comping voices, generally played softer than the ride cymbal. The function of the ride cymbal now features rhythmic development as opposed to the static ride pattern played in earlier styles. Additionally, the hi-hat is no longer tied to the traditional 2 and 4 beats. This style is more open and forward-moving than previous styles.

In order to move forward in this style, a short review is needed to ensure accuracy between the limbs. I find that practicing quarter notes on the ride cymbal is an excellent way to ensure an even and equidistant pulse that can later be internalized. I believe it would be beneficial to review the traditional jazz ride pattern with accents on beats 2 and 4 before moving onto the accents on the "and" of beats 2 and 4.

Begin by playing quarter notes, then swing eighth notes and then triplets on the snare drum beneath the ride pattern. Continue by repeating these exercises with the bass drum. This ensures that the ride pattern is consistent as well as locking in the snare drum and bass drum to it.

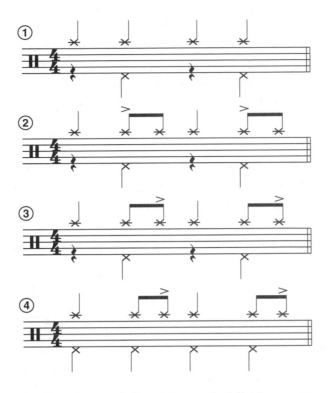

Try playing the following rhythms beneath the ride-cymbal/hi-hat patterns.

These examples should be played with both accented ride-cymbal patterns.

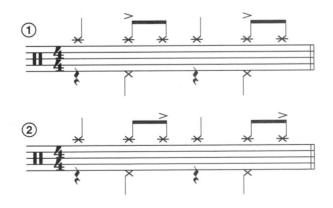

Resolution Points

Resolution Points (also known as "Turnarounds") are phrase endings that act as markers in the form. For example, beat "1" is a traditional resolution point, used to mark the form after playing eight measures. It is a good idea to expand the resolution points to open up the music and make it sound less predictable. I have incorporated four other beats that can be used to replace beat "1." They are "4-and," "4," "1-and," and "2." In the following exercise, you can play four-measure, eight-measure or twelve-measure examples of improvised time with comping and end the phrases with each of these five resolution points.

CHAPTER 1:
Alternating Ride-Cymbal Patterns

This section deals with deleting various upbeats that are normally associated with a traditional ride pattern. By taking away a note, the ride pattern is more open. The hi-hat can be played lightly on beats 2 and 4 in these exercises.

Deletions [2-and/4-and]

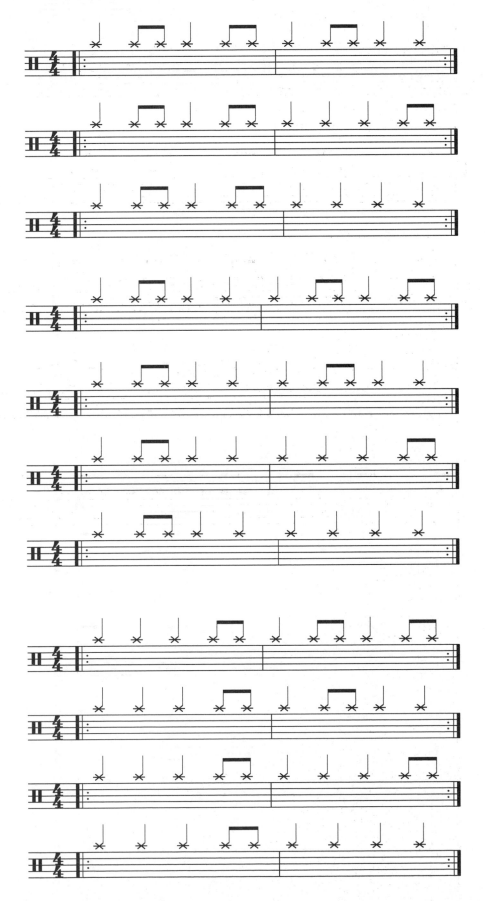

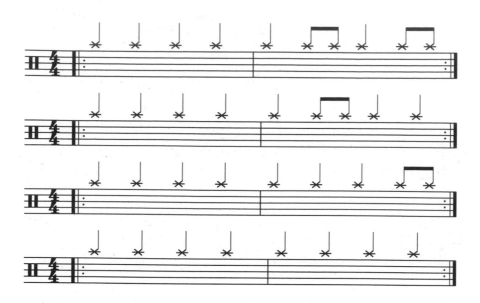

Play-along with the $\frac{4}{4}$ swing CD tracks 20 and 24.

Ties (2-and/4-and)

This section deals with tying upbeat 2-and or 4-and to the following downbeat, thus alternating the ride-cymbal pattern.

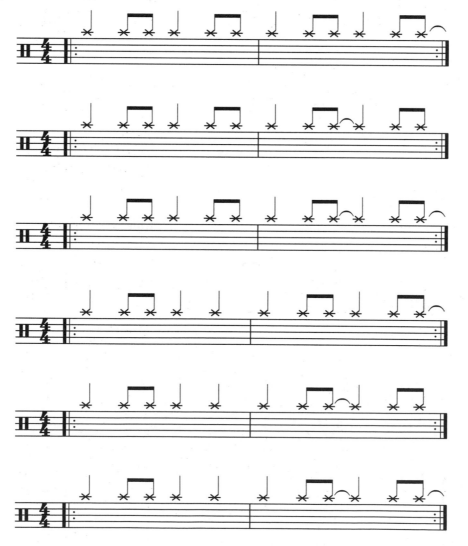

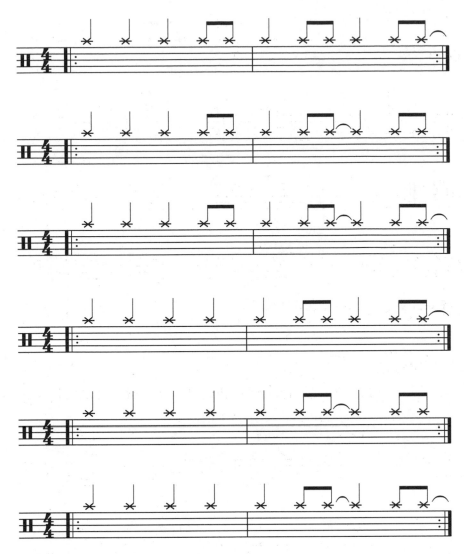

Play along with the $\frac{4}{4}$ swing CD tracks 20 and 24.

Additions [1-and/3-and]

This section deals with adding 1-and and 3-and to the ride pattern in order to alternate it.

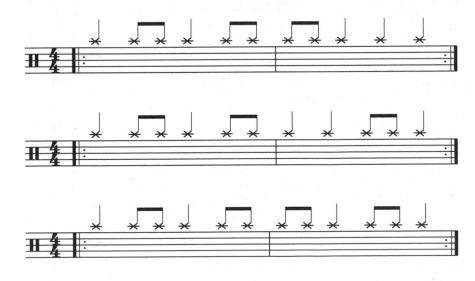

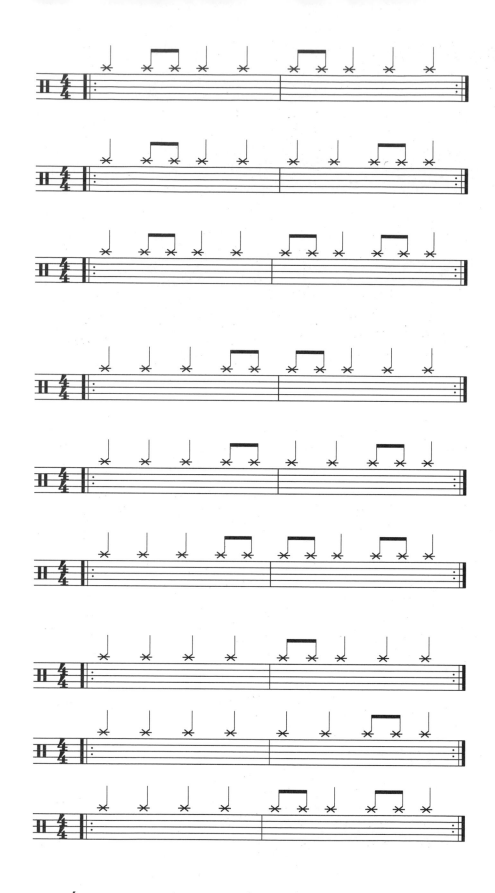

Play along with the $\frac{4}{4}$ swing CD tracks 20 and 24.

Ties (1-and/3-and)

This section deals with adding a tie to the upbeats 1-and / 3-and.

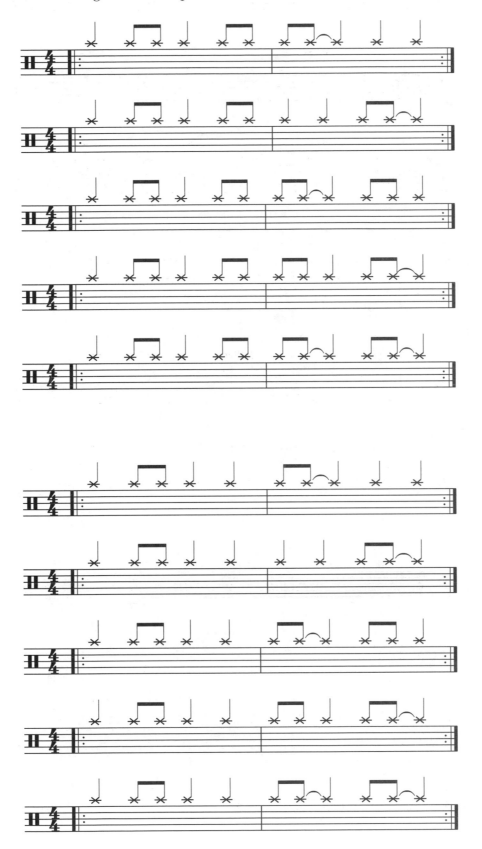

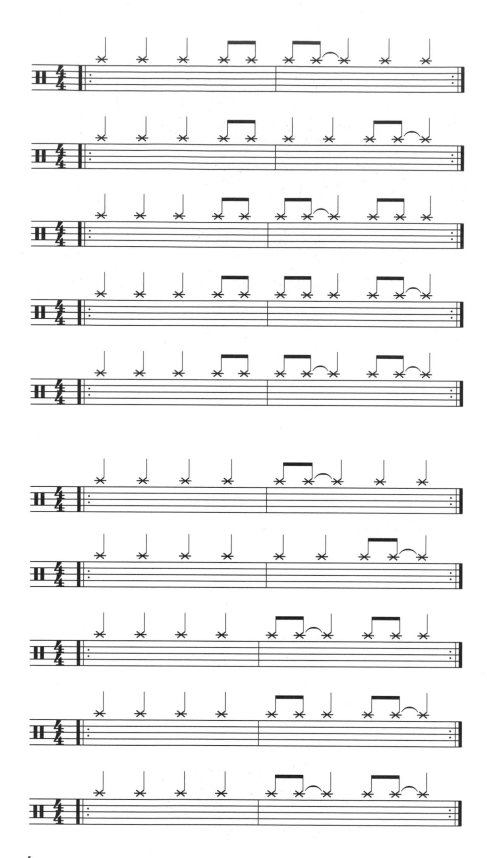

Play along with $\frac{4}{4}$ swing CD tracks 20 and 24.

Combinations: Selected Examples

The following examples combine the use of deletions, additions and ties from the previous pages.

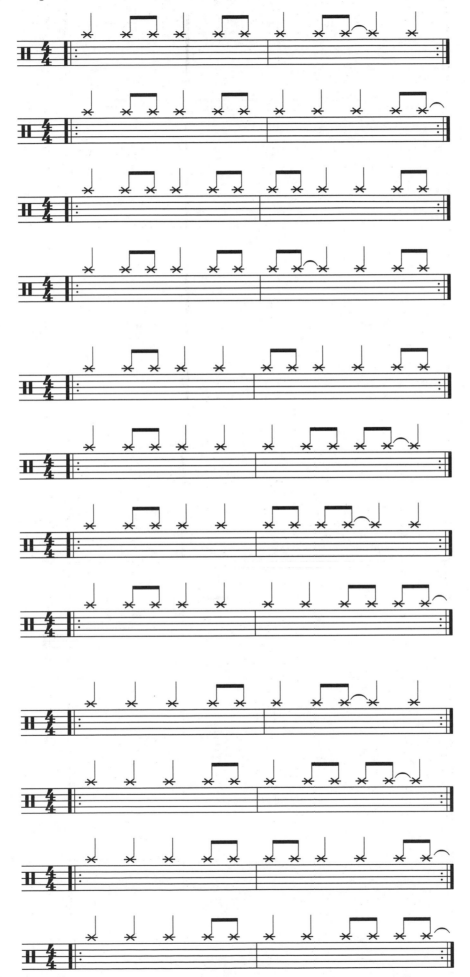

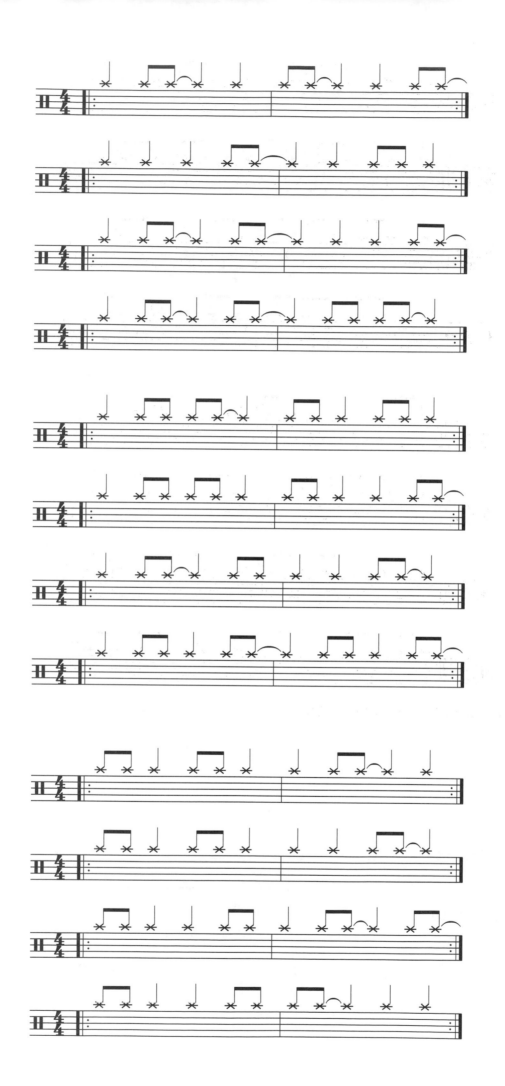

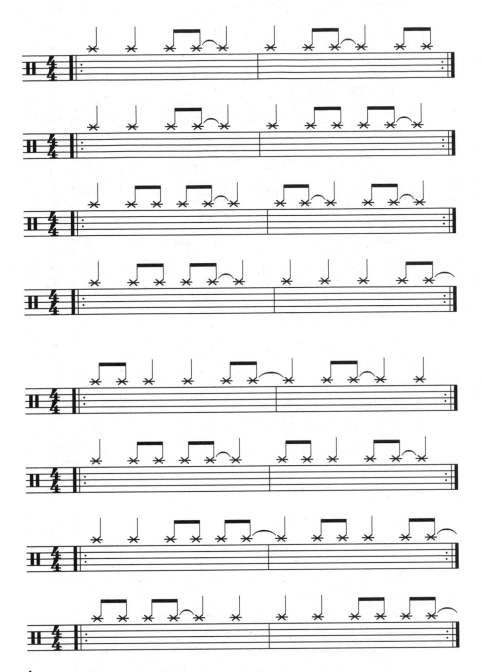

Play along with $\frac{4}{4}$ swing CD tracks 20 and 24.

The Hi-Hat

This section deals with the concept of relieving the hit-hat of the restriction of playing on beats 2 and 4. Just as the ride cymbal can alternate its pattern and phrase rhythms, the hi-hat can get away from the 2 and 4 ostinato. Starting with "deletions," remove various 2's and 4's from an improvised time feel:

After deleting some hi-hat notes, there is more room for "additions," or notes that can be added by the hi-hat. For this exercise, add some 1's and 3's to the improvised ride pattern.

By "deleting" and "adding" to the hi-hat, the impression is given that the hi-hat is more active than it actually is.

CHAPTER 2:
Comping

1. Practice each beat separately on the snare drum, bass drum and hi-hat; first with the traditional ride beat, then with an alternate beat. Play the hi-hat on beats 2 and 4.
2. Combine various upbeats and downbeats separately on the snare drum, bass drum and hi-hat.
3. Improvise multiple notes—upbeats and downbeats—between the snare drum, bass drum and hi-hat.

Play along with $\frac{4}{4}$ swing CD tracks 20 and 24.

Alternate Ride and Comping Together

Play lower part on snare or bass drum.
Play the hi-hat on beats 2 and 4, then improvise the hi-hat part.

Play along with $\frac{4}{4}$ swing CD tracks 20 and 24.

CHAPTER 3:
¾ Swing

The traditional pattern

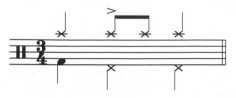

became

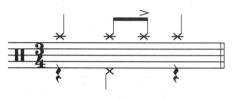

Introduce a dotted-quarter feeling:

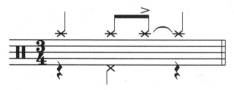

relates to:

The contemporary ¾ feel has a feeling of a dotted quarter or swing 2 against 3. The tied "and of 2" makes this feel work.

¾ Alternating Ride-Cymbal Patterns

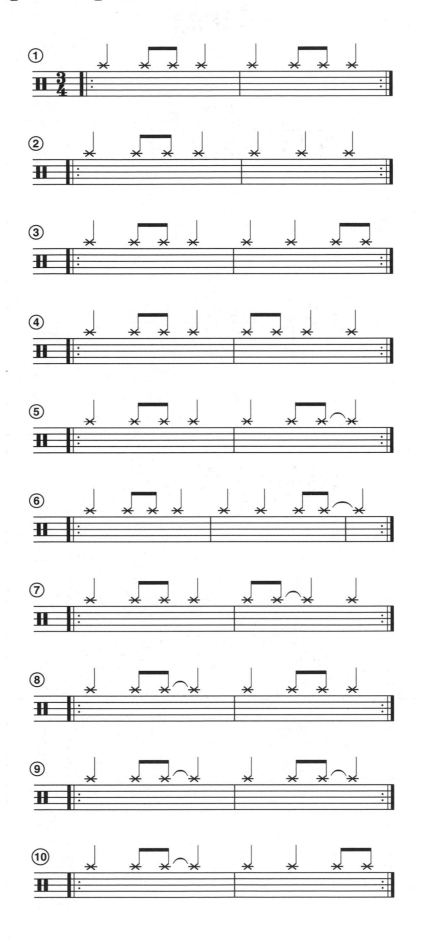

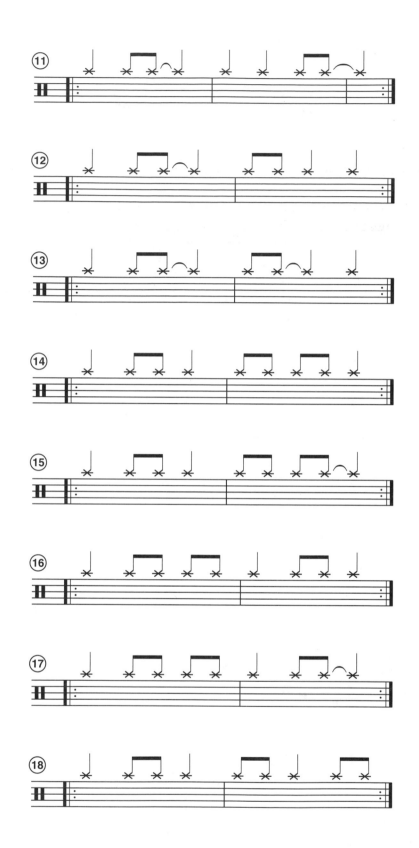

Play along with $\frac{3}{4}$ swing CD track 22.

¾ Comping

Start by using the following ride pattern,

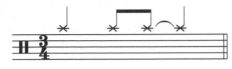

then try other patterns.

1. Practice comping each beat separately on the snare drum, bass drum and hi-hat. Play the hi-hat on beat 2 when not comping.
2. Practice multiple beats separately on the snare drum, bass drum and hi-hat.
3. Practice multiple upbeats and downbeats between the snare drum, bass drum and hi-hat.

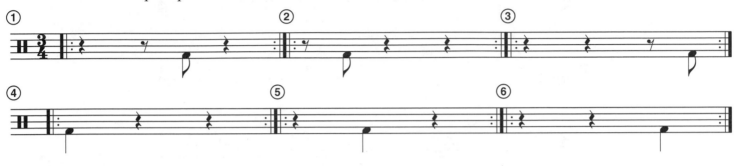

Play along with ¾ swing CD track 22.

¾ Alternating Ride and Comping Together

Play lower part on snare or bass drum. Play the hi-hat on beat 2, then improvise the hi-hat part.

Play along with ¾ swing CD track 22.

CHAPTER 4:
Straight Eighths, ECM Style

In the 1970s and 80s, the European record label ECM (Edition of Contemporary Music) developed an improvised Jazz style based on straight eighths. Here are some examples.

Selected Ride Patterns

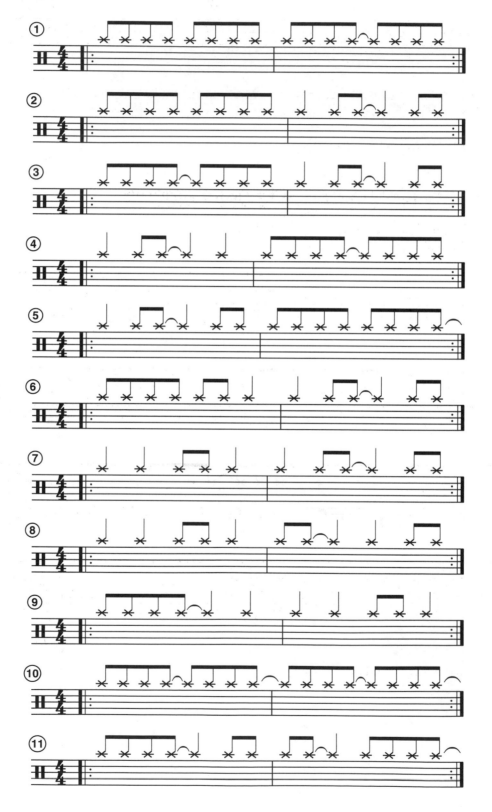

Play along with straight-eighth CD track 26.

Straight Eighths, Comping

Once again, this comping uses the snare drum, bass drum and hi-hat as equal comping voices to support the alternating ride pattern.

Comp using the eighth notes mixed between the voices under the improvised ride cymbal. Start with a single note; then use multiple notes to create rhythmic phrases.

Play along with straight-eighth CD track 26.

Straight Eighths Alternating Ride and Comping

Play lower part on snare drum, bass drum or hi-hat.

Play along with straight-eighth CD track 26.

PLAY-ALONG TRACKS:

4/4 Blues Tune
CD Track #19 (Demo)/#20 (Play-along)

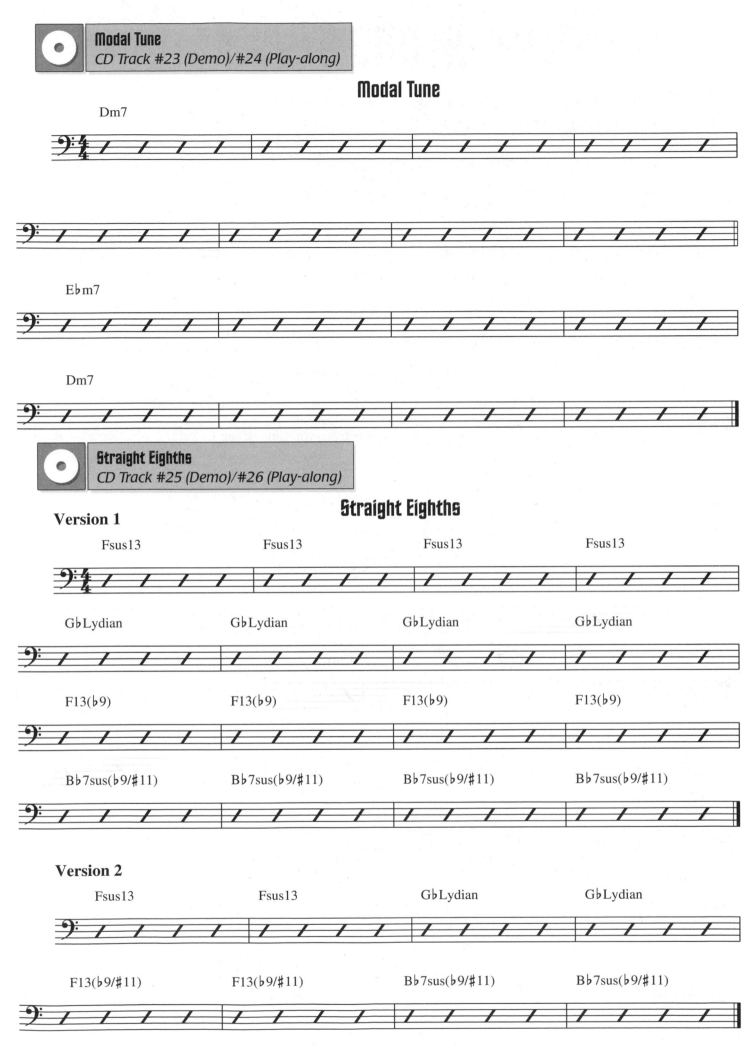

Selected Discography

Blade, Brian	Night and Day (from Kenny Garret *Triology*)
Chambers, Joe	Footprints (Wayne Shorter *Adam's Apple*)
	Mode for Joe (Joe Henderson *Mode for Joe*)
Cobb, Jimmy	So What? (Miles Davis *Kind of Blue*)
	All Blues (from Miles Davis *Kind of Blue*)
DeJohnette, Jack	Bye-Bye Blackbird (Keith Jarret *Bye-Bye Blackbird*)
	Gazelle (Dave Liebman *Trio Plus One*)
	Nothing Personal (Michael Brecker *Michael Brecker*)
Haynes, Roy	If I Should Lose You (Roy Haynes *Out of the Afternoon*)
	Matrix (Chick Corea *Now He Sings, Now He Sobs*)
	Question and Answer (Pat Metheney *Question and Answer*)
Jones, Elvin	Chim Chim Cheree (John Coltrane *Chim Chim Cheree*)
	Crescent (John Coltrane *Crescent*)
	My Favorite Things (John Coltrane *My Favorite Things*)
	One Down, One Up (John Coltrane *Dear Old Stockholm*)
	Resolution (John Coltrane *A Love Supreme*)
	Transition (John Coltrane *Transition*)
	Wild Flower (Wayne Shorter *Speak No Evil*)
Stewart, Bill	Big Fan (John Scofield *Meant to Be*)
	Valse Hot (Larry Goldings *Light Blue*)
Watts, Jeff	Spartacus (Branford Marsalis *Crazy People Music*)
Williams, Tony	All Blues (Miles Davis *My Funny Valentine 1964*)
	Cantaloupe Island (Herbie Hancock *Empyrean Isles*)
	Delores (Miles Davis *Miles Smiles*)
	Footprints (Miles Davis *Miles Smiles*)
	Maiden Voyage (Herbie Hancock *Maiden Voyage*)
	Seven Steps to Heaven (Miles Davis *Seven Steps to Heaven*)
	So What? (Miles Davis *Four and More*)

thecollective
Contemporary Styles Series

BOOKS WITH CDs

The material in The Collective Contemporary Styles Series represents many years of work on the part of many talented Collective faculty members, who have the experience of playing and teaching these styles to literally thousands of young rhythm-section musicians over the last thirty years. This series is the fruit of their labor and talent with the information presented in a manner that is easy to grasp.

CO1 **Afro-Caribean & Brazilian Rhythms for the Drums**
By Memo Acevedo, Frank Katz, Chris Lacinak, Kim Plainfield, Adrian Santos, and Maciek Schijbal

CO2 **Afro-Caribean & Brazilian Rhythms for the Bass**
By Lincoln Goines, Steve Marks, Nilson Matta, Irio O'Farill and Leo Traversa

CO3 **Fusion: A Study in Contemporary Music for the Drums**
By Kim Plainfield

CO4 **Fusion: A Study in Contemporary Music for the Bass**
By Leo Traversa

CO5 **Contemporary Rock Styles for the Drums**
By Sandy Gennaro

CO6 **Contemporary Rock Styles for the Bass**
By Gary Kelly

CO7 **Contemporary Jazz Styles for the Drums**
By Ian Froman and Peter Retzlaff

CO8 **Contemporary Jazz Styles for the Bass**
By Joe Fitzgerald and Hilliard Greene

CO9 **The Roots of Groove: R&B/Soul & Contemporary R&B and Funk Styles for the Drums**
By Pat Petrillo

CO10 **Contemporary R&B and Funk Styles for the Bass**
By Frank Gravis and Steve Marks

CO11 **Contemporary Hip Hop and Drum 'n' Bass Styles for the Drums**
By Guy Licata

CO12 **Contemporary Hip Hop and Drum 'n' Bass Styles for the Bass**
By John Davis

CARL FISCHER
MUSIC